The Power To Love Workbook

AuthorHouse™
1663 Liberty Drive
Bloomington, IN 47403
www.authorhouse.com
Phone: 1-800-839-8640

First published by AuthorHouse   6/30/2010

ISBN: 978-1-4520-3768-4 (e)
ISBN: 978-1-4520-3767-7 (sc)

Printed in the United States of America
Bloomington, Indiana

This book is printed on acid-free paper.

Dedications

I would like to thank my wife Karen for her love and help for the 25 plus years we have been married. She loves me enough to enable me to dedicate time and effort to this ministry and well as others. She is a God send and a great example of how to love even when the going gets tough and in overcoming personal desires and living in a sacrificial manner.

I love her with all my heart and thank God for bringing her to me every day.

How to Use This Book

The power to love God and others is impossible apart from the Gospel of Jesus Christ. On our own we can barely love those who love us much less those who don't! It is the good news of God's amazing love for us that gives us the power to love him back and to love others with his divine love. In "The Power to Love" we discover many concepts and techniques that enable us to develop the skills necessary to love others.

As a companion to "Power to Love" by John Glenn this workbook allows the reader to give some thought to the concepts within the textbook in order to develop and practice the skills needed to love others like Christ. Each of the chapters corresponds to the chapters in the text book and each question emphasizes a relevant concept or principle discussed in the text. The reader is encouraged to answer the questions in the work book by putting the concepts of the text into their own words. This process will insure a better understanding as well as application in your own life.

No question requires an answer for you to generate based upon your own opinion. But you should feel free to interject as you see fit. Once you read the chapter, turn to the workbook and think about the questions and then refer to the textbook to check your answers. You may disagree with certain points, but please think about why and trust the Spirit of God to guide you into all truth. You may also use the workbook as a guide to teaching through the textbook or leading a small group. Be aware the workbook does not cover every concept within the textbook and in using it this way; you may well want to include the issues that God brings to your mind as well as those within the workbook. Most of all, this workbook is for you. May God bless your efforts to learn how to love others.

Contents

I. Foundations: The Critical Event

Turning the Relational Corner

What is the primary relationship? And Why?

_____

_____

_____

_____

What is the best biblical term for relational empowerment?

_____

_____

What is the critical event?

_____

_____

To what extent are we able to love others?

_____

_____

_____

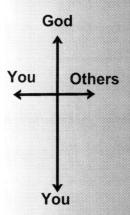

1 John 4:6-7
Beloved, let us love one another, for love is of God, and everyone who loves has been born of God, and knows God.
The one who does not love has not known God. For God is love.

What two conditions must be met in order to love others?

1. ....

....

2. ....

....

The change in identity brought by God through his Spirit is called what?

....

What does God do to bring about this change in identity?

....

....

What does "knowing" God really entail?

....

....

To know God intimately involves two concepts. What are they?

1. ....

....

2. ....

....

What are two provisions does God provide to meet our need for security and significance?

1. ....

2. ....

How are our deepest needs for love and respect satisfied?

....

....

Relational Empowerment Goals

What signifies ones spiritual condition?

....

....

Why was Paul unable to speak to the Corinthians as spiritually mature?

....

....

....

....

What did Paul mean by the "milk" of the word?

....

....

What did Paul mean by the "meat" of the word?

....

....

How is God impressed by us?

_____

_____

_____

In order to mature spiritually and practice the critical event, what is necessary?

_____

_____

Before trying to reach out to and love others it is necessary to consider our own condition.   How do we do this?

_____

_____

_____

How is forgiveness a two-way street? (Be careful).

_____

_____

Relational Empowerment Skills

Relational empowerment involves learning and practicing three sets of skills (personal skills, communication skills, and relational skills) on a daily basis.

The first set is referred to as personal skills. Fill in the blanks.

- Cognitive Restructuring

    o _____

- Emotional Management

  o ....

- Behavioral Redirection

  o ....

- Spiritual Enlightenment

  o ....

The next set is Communication Skills. List them.

1. ....
2. ....
3. ....
4. ....

The final set is Relational Skills. Fill in the blanks.

- Warn the unruly

  o ....

- Comfort the hurting

  o ....

- Support the weak in the faith

  o ....

The relational skills are true expressions of divine love that share what characteristics?

2. Cognitive Restructuring

Personal Skills Needed for Our Relationship to God

Before we try to understand what we should say or how we should behave when loving others what must we do?

What is the answer to above called?

Many Christians may understand that God is supposed to love them, or even that he has loved them both intellectually and theologically; but they are not at all convinced that he really does love them personally. What reveals this?

Where do we find the strength to relate to others?

Relational Skills

1. <u>Cognitive restructuring</u> Changing our thinking about ourselves.
2. <u>Emotional management</u> Controlling our own feelings.
3. <u>Behavioral redirection</u> Changing our motives from manipulation to ministry.
4. <u>Spiritual enlightenment</u> Listening to the inner voice of God.

The inability to practice these relational skills results in what?

Repentance: 180 Degree Change in Thinking

Define Cognitive Restructuring.

Since the cross, what is sin?

Define repentance.

Through repentance, how do we see ourselves?

When Peter called his contemporaries to repentance he was speaking to what?

_____

_____

_____

Changing Core Beliefs About Ourselves

What is the root of relational difficulties?

_____

_____

_____

In a personal sense, what is as important as the air we breathe?

_____

_____

To be secure and significant as a person, what must we know and believe?

_____

_____

_____

Because of our union with Christ, what do we share with him?

_____

_____

_____

Each day we have a choice as to what we are going to believe about ourselves. What is that choice?

_____

_____

What is the basic faulty assumption?

_____

_____

Replacing Lies with Truth

What is the correct assumption?

_____

_____

Robert McGee, the author of *The Search for Significance.* In his book he list four "lies" about our worth as persons that are common to all.   What are they?

1. _____

2. _____

3. _____

4. _____

Robert McGee also lists four false assumptions.   What are they?

1. _____

2. _____

3. _____

4. _____

List the spiritual blessings Paul cites in Ephesians Chapter 1.

In order to continually avoid these false assumptions, what is it we must constantly rehearse?

As we look into the "mirror" of God's Word, what is it we must see?

3. Emotional Management

Empowered to Love

What is the false assumption the disciples had that hindered them from loving each other?

....

....

....

What must we do in order to love others like Christ?

....

....

....

The Key to Emotional Management

All of us have been conditioned to believe that we should feel bad when bad things happen to us. What is the truth?

....

....

....

Notes

He had just reveled to them that he was leaving them.

How do we control what we feel?

What is the role of the Holy Spirit regarding our emotions?

Finish these sentences:

Rather than allowing our selves to slip into hatred:

Instead of simply feeling sorry for ourselves when we are hurt:

Instead of becoming anxious:

The good news about believers is that they really are secure in God's love and significant in God's plan if they maintain their relationship with God.

Is the above statement true or false? Explain.

What is the reason we are encouraged to "count it all joy" when we face bad times?

What do We Believe?

What is the Old Covenant mind set when it comes to suffering?

What are the three points of the eternal view of suffering?

1.

2.

3.

What is emotional management?

How did Jesus demonstrate emotional management?

What to do with Hurt Feelings

What two terms are used to describe the natural way of handling our emotions? Describe each.

D

S

What are the three parts of emotional management?

1. ....

....

2. ....

....

3. ....

....

What surprises us when we commit to serving others regard-less of how we feel?

....

....

....

4. Behavioral Redirection

Ministry or Manipulation

Define Ministry.

Notes

Healthy	Dysfunctional
Faith	Fear
Hope	Pride
Love	Guilt

Define Manipulation.

What are two key questions about what we do?

What major justification do we often use to seek our own benefit within the disguise of helping others?

Often in order to feel worthy our true motivation for our behavior is?

Why is it necessary to ask God to reveal the true motivation behind our motivation?

Define a true goal of ministry?

Recognition of Motives

Describe the personal skill of behavior redirection.

What does 1 John 1:5-9 mean by "walk in the light"?

What is the natural tendency to identify ourselves?

Although we have been spiritually transformed into the image of Christ, what is our problem?

What is God's concern about our behavior?

In 1 Corinthians 3, what is the difference between wood, hay and stubble, and gold, silver and precious stones?

The Miracle of Change

As we focus on our new identity in Christ what happens?

As we practice the Miracle of Change, what is:

Our responsibility?

_____

_____

God's responsibility?

_____

_____

Breaking the Hurt-Hate-Hurt Cycle

What is the Hurt-Hate-Hurt Cycle?

_____

_____

_____

What is the greatest need of behavioral motivation?

_____

_____

_____

In our efforts to cope with resentment, bitterness and hatred, what do we do?

_____

_____

_____

The actual process of eliminating internal hatred begins with what?

What must we recognize about our hatred towards others who have hurt us?

What do we have to do to be able to love others?

What was Jesus' response to those who hated him?

Summary

Loving others like Christ is far more than trying to develop and maintain good manners and live up to a moral code that is acceptable to God and others.

Why?

5. Spiritual Enlightenment

What is Spiritual Enlightenment?

What is meant by Spiritual enlightenment?

1.

2.

What was Jesus' new commandment and promise?

What does the Spirit, in his role as comforter do for us?

Spiritual enlightenment reveals what two factors regarding change?

_____

_____

_____

The Promise of the Spirit

Why must we all suffer?

_____

_____

_____

What is the connection between the personal skill of enlightenment and suffering?

_____

_____

_____

What is a primary role of the Holy Spirit?

_____

_____

_____

What made Jesus so healthy and able to function so well in this world?

_____

_____

_____

How does this apply to us?

_____

_____

_____

After describing his agonizing struggle in Romans 7, what does Paul reveal?

_____

_____

The heart of spiritual enlightenment involves what?

_____

_____

What is Christ actualization?

_____

_____

The Leadership of the Spirit

In Romans 8:14-17, what does Paul describe?

_____

_____

_____

Romans 8:14-17

For as many as are led by *the* Spirit of God, they are the sons of God.

For you have not received the spirit of bondage again to fear, but you have received the Spirit of adoption by which we cry, Abba, Father!

The Spirit Himself bears witness with our spirit that we are the children of God.

And if we are children, then we are heirs; heirs of God and joint-heirs with Christ; so that if we suffer with *Him*, we may also be glorified together.

What two kinds of motivations are contrasted?

How are they characterized?

How will we relate to God following the personal leadership of the indwelling Spirit?

List three factors to consider when hearing from God.

What is the means that gives meaning to these factors?

What is the spirit of adoption?

How does our experience of security and significance become real?

The Fullness of the Spirit

The text in Ephesians 5:18 is written in three nuances of Greek. What do they indicate?

How do we grieve the Spirit?

How do we quench the Spirit?

_____

_____

_____

Instead of grieving or quenching the Spirit, what are we to do?

_____

_____

The Renewing of the Mind

How is the skill of personal enlightenment a matter of what regarding renewing the mind?

_____

_____

The renewing of the minds is a one-time event. True of false?

Explain.

_____

_____

What is our part in renewing our minds?

_____

_____

How is this described in 2 Corinthians 3:18?

....

....

....

Summary

What difficulty do we encounter as we recognize God working in and through us?

....

....

....

6. Spirituality Not Religiosity

Give examples of religious ways to be spiritual.

Define religion.

Define true spirituality.

What does the blinding power of Satan also known as the core of religiosity attempt to do?

Define religiosity.

_____

_____

_____

Why is spirituality more fundamental than the various religions in which it is found?

_____

_____

_____

_____

Authentic Faith Verses Toxic faith

Define toxic faith.

_____

_____

_____

Define authentic faith.

_____

_____

_____

Where is toxic faith focused?

_____

_____

Where is authentic faith focused?

....

....

What does toxic faith worry about?

....

....

What opposite characteristics demonstrate authentic faith?

....

....

How is authentic faith expressed?

....

....

How is toxic faith expressed?

....

....

Toxic Faith and Religious Addiction

Give examples of religious addiction.

_____

_____

_____

List some common behaviors of the religious addict.

_____

_____

What does the religious addict use to find relief?

_____

_____

_____

What are the often missed underlying motives of the religious addict?

_____

_____

_____

What foundational idea make the toxic faith system so toxic?

Toxic faith may be broken down into three categories. What are they.

1.

2.

3.

What is the root of religious addiction?

Authentic Faith and Out Identity

In our natural state for what is the best we can hope?

The intensity of personal suffering drives us to what?

Am I Good or Bad?

According to the text, what is the "ruler" to which Christians refer?

_____

What is the main problem with biblical interpretation?

_____

_____

_____

What are two methods of interpretation?

1. _____

2. _____

Depending upon the interpretation method used, how is human nature viewed?

_____

_____

_____

_____

_____

What is the key to answering the question of "Am I good or bad?"

_____

_____

_____

Why is the task of making ourselves good so impossible?

_____

_____

_____

"Born again" refers to what?

_____

_____

_____

Done by who?

_____

How is authentic faith expressed?

_____

_____

_____

What kind of interpretation of the Bible will result in toxic faith?

....

....

....

Am I Religious or Spiritual?

Why do religious addicts turn to religious activities?

....

....

....

What are some examples of how false assumptions may be switched from the secular to the sacred?

....

....

....

....

....

Explain how different spiritual enlightenment is from addictive religious activity.

....

....

....

As a result of believing their new and real identity what experience follows?

_____

_____

_____

The text describes a cycle of emptiness that occurs when the question of "I will be worthy if..." is answered incorrectly. Describe this cycle.

_____

_____

_____

What is the proper view of the Bible?

_____

What is the improper view of the Bible?

_____

Summary

What are the three things Jesus said about toxic religious leaders.

1. _____

2. _____

3. _____

7. Communication Skills – The Miracle of Communication

What are some typical statements that indicate problems with communication?

....

....

....

The Word

In his gospel the Apostle John refers to Jesus as "the Word." In the context of the textbook what does this signify?

....

....

....

In terms of communication, besides being a means of communication what else is Jesus?

....

....

....

Why must our vertical communication with God precede our horizontal communication with others?

....

....

....

The Communication Process

What are two broad categories of communication?

1. ....
2. ....

With whom does the responsibility of transmission lie?

....

Why?

....

....

....

What is relational noise?

....

....

Explain the implication that we are born with two ears and one mouth?

....

....

....

Give some common examples of not listening actively.

....

....

....

....

....

What is one way to inaccurately interpret a statement?

....

....

....

What means can be used to avoid the problem of interpretation?

....

....

....

What are the two fundamental and obvious requirements for true communication?

1. ....

....

....

2. ....

....

The Miracle of Communication

What example given in the Book of Acts illustrates the miracle of communication?

_____

_____

_____

Why did Jesus tell his disciples not to worry about what to say?

_____

_____

The Apostle John refers to Jesus as "the word" in the context of these lessons what does this signify?

_____

_____

_____

What is more important than eloquent speech in effective communication?

_____

_____

_____

In addition to being a method of communication what else is Jesus?

Why must our vertical communication with God precede our horizontal communication with others?

Summary

How does the Spirit of God enable true communication regarding our motivation?

8. Communication Skills –
Speaking the Truth in Love

Ministry or Manipulation?

What groupings of emotions determines how well or not so well our communication is received?

_____

_____

_____

What is corrupt communication?

_____

_____

_____

What are the most typical lies we tell ourselves?

_____

_____

_____

_____

How does this spill over to others?

_____

_____

_____

We have a natural tendency to evaluate the worth of others in the same way we do ourselves and typically confuse their behavior or circumstances with their identity. What results from this?

_____

_____

_____

What is the only means of not lying?

_____

_____

Life Words or Death Words

What are the two main goals of personal skills?

_____

_____

_____

_____

What is the only way personal communication can be received by the listener?

What are "death" words?

What are "life" words?

How do we avoid the selfishness and pride that is so natural in our communication?

What is the faith that produces a hope in the future?

Time Out for the Trip In

Typically we try to communicate based upon what?

_____

_____

_____

What happens when arguments escalate?

_____

_____

_____

During the trip in what do we discover?

_____

_____

_____

What time commitment and scheduling is necessary for the trip in?

_____

_____

_____

When we are actually "walking in the Light as he is in the light" what are we doing?

....

....

....

....

Changing from the Inside Out

The renewing of the mind is a biblical term for what?

....

....

....

....

Regarding the renewing of the mind, what is the work of the Comforter?

....

....

....

What are the characteristics of the mind of Christ?

Why did Jesus see the need for his baptism?

What is genuine humility?

Why is this characteristic absolutely vital in active listening?

What hinders us in complete submission and obedience to the will of the Father?

....

....

....

Why can the carnal mind not perceive exultation and glory of God?

....

....

....

Summary

What are the two aspects of speaking the truth in love?

....

....

9. Communication Skills – What to Talk About

Core Issues

Describe core issues.

_____

_____

_____

Describe superficial issues.

_____

_____

_____

Upon what do all issues hinge?

_____

_____

_____

As parents, what should we talk about with our children?

_____

_____

When parents speak to their children how do the get the cart before the horse?

How do both husbands and wives fail to communicate with their spouses?

Husband?

Wife?

What overlap in needs applies to both men and women?

Regarding children, what does it mean to "bring them up in the nurture and admiration of the Lord"?

Letting God Talk

What two factors take a lot of faith?

1. _____

2. _____

Based upon these two factors and the accompanying faith what does communication at this level mean?

_____

_____

_____

What should <u>not</u> be done when talking about core issues?

_____

_____

What is just as important as to know what to talk about?

_____

What is the 30 second rule?

_____

_____

What determines the quality of our emotions?

_____

_____

All too often we treat other people's feelings like a bag full of stinky garbage…we do or say anything just to get rid of them. What are some typical ways to reject the feelings of others?

_____

_____

_____

_____

How do we demonstrate acceptance of another's feelings?

_____

_____

_____

Actions Speak Louder than Words

Describe modeling.

_____

_____

_____

_____

Explain double-bind messages.

_____

_____

_____

Double-bind messages come from what?

....

....

....

How can non-verbal cues be part of a double-bind message?

....

....

....

The Blessing

When considering what to talk about in our communication, what is most important?

....

....

....

What is one of the most subtle traps of the enemy?

....

....

....

What is the ultimate goal of communication with others?

....

....

....

How do we demonstrate the Gospel regarding the worth of others?

_____

_____

_____

Where is the communication skill of the blessing most needed?

_____

_____

What is the most basic purpose of personal relationships?

_____

_____

_____

Summary

What do Jesus' words, "For out of the abundance of the heart, the mouth speaks" mean in our everyday conversations?

_____

_____

_____

With what should the blessing not be confused?

_____

_____

_____

10. Relational Ministry

What is the critical event which we must exercise as the foundation to relational ministry?

_____

_____

Warn the Unruly

Who are the unruly?

_____

_____

What is the basic idea regarding warning the unruly?

_____

_____

_____

What is the only way to change someone's thinking?

_____

_____

_____

1 Thessalonians 5:14

Now we exhort you, brethren, warn them that are unruly, comfort the feebleminded, support the weak...

Galatians 6:1

Brethren, if a man be overtaken in a fault, ye which are spiritual, restore such a one in the spirit of meekness; considering thyself, lest thou also be tempted.

2 Corinthians

Blessed be God, even the Father of our Lord Jesus Christ, the Father of mercies, and the God of all comfort; Who comforteth us in all our tribulation, that we may be able to comfort them which are in any trouble, by the comfort wherewith we ourselves are comforted of God.

Restoration involves what?

Regarding ourselves, what does warning the unruly demand?

Warning the unruly requires what?

Who is charged with the responsibility of being used by God to confront and restore those who are not behaving appropriately.

Confront the Feeble Minded

Who are the feebleminded?

What offers more comfort than eloquent speech?

Why do we not enjoy being with people who are hurting?

Support the Weak

Who are the weak?

What is the telltale sign of the weak?

As a result of the telltale sign, what do the weak do?

Why is it that our natural reaction to the weak is to avoid them at all costs?

_____

_____

_____

How do the weak identify themselves?

_____

_____

What kind of role do they like to play?

_____

_____

What are doubtful issues?

_____

_____

_____

What do the weak in faith do about them?

_____

_____

_____

What is the difficult part of supporting those who are weak?

....

....

....

Accepting the weak as worthy persons despite their religious and obnoxious flesh is sometimes a real challenge. How do we do this?

....

....

....

Summary

What is our goal in life?

....

....

....

II. Confrontation without Condemnation

Introduction

Jesus knew that living in a sin-cursed body that still has the flesh, with others who also have the flesh, was not going to be easy. In that context Jesus went on to teach his disciples what?

How is this done and what does it mean?

When to Confront? - Timing

What is the first issue to consider when confronting another?

What is the most critical point in preparing to confront another?

_____

_____

_____

The key phrase in Paul's command to restore the one overtaken in a fault is, "you who are spiritual restore such a one..." What does this mean?

_____

_____

_____

What risk do we run if we do not recognize this spiritual component?

_____

_____

_____

Why Confront? - Motivation

List the ten questions we must ask ourselves before we confront an unruly person.

1. _____

2. _____

3. _____

4. _____

5. _____

6. _____

8. _____

9. _____

10. _____

What do we need to talk to God about before we talk to others?

_____

_____

_____

Why?

_____

_____

_____

Most likely the unruly behavior will present a threat to our own sense of worth causing us to doubt our own security and significance. How does this doubt neutralize us?

_____

_____

_____

How does the "trip in" help us?

_____

_____

_____

What is the one thing Earl had to realize before he could get well?

....

....

Restoration or Condemnation?

What do we use as the means to condemn rather than restore?

....

....

Why is this a hurtful and ineffective approach?

....

....

What is a key point about our commitment regarding confrontation?

....

....

Behavioral Modification is not Enough

What is the initial goal of confrontation?

....

....

....

Most people, especially children, are not aware of their own personal needs for unconditional love and genuine respect. Of what else are the unruly unaware?

....

....

....

Unless what, why is any observable change temporary?

....

....

....

The Identity Factor

What is the goal of restoration?

....

....

....

Statements like, "This proves that you are nothing but a thief!" will do nothing but reinforce the behavior of shoplifting. What is the better alternative?

Replacing a false identification with the new and true identification requires what two things?

1.

2.

What two examples are given that express confrontational love and "tough" love?

1.

2.

Why is it important to listen to the Spirit in these examples and other situations of life?

12. Comfort without Enabling

The Call to Comfort

When Paul refers to God as "Father..." what does this imply?

_____

_____

_____

We receive comfort from God for what purpose?

_____

_____

_____

Because of our union with Christ, what do we understand?

_____

_____

_____

What is revealed in the first half of Romans 8?

_____

_____

_____

_____

Romans 8:17
And if we are children, then we are heirs; heirs of God and joint-heirs with Christ; so that if we suffer with *Him*, we may also be glorified together.

Romans 5:1-5
Therefore being justified by faith, we have peace with God through our Lord Jesus Christ.

Through Him we also have access by faith into this grace in which we stand, and we rejoice on the hope of the glory of God.

And not only *this*, but we glory in afflictions also, knowing that afflictions work out patience,

and patience *works out* experience, and experience *works out* hope.

And hope does not make *us* ashamed, because the love of God has been poured out in our hearts through *the* Holy Spirit given to us.

In verse 17, what connection does Paul make?

The Eternal View of Suffering

Why can we actually glory or rejoice in our tribulations instead of dreading them?

What is the eternal view of suffering?

Why should we not be surprised when we suffer?

What is a religious deal?

84

Why is obedience not a way to avoid suffering?

....

....

....

Why must we first be comforted by God to be able to comfort others?

....

....

....

Comforting Others

The most difficult part of comforting others is that we must learn to accept rather than reject their hurt feelings. What does this mean?

....

....

....

....

When comforting others, it is usually far more important to do what?

....

....

....

Recall the ABC Theory of Emotions.

_____

_____

_____

_____

What is the main goal in helping others with their security and significance?

_____

_____

True comfort comes from only where?

_____

_____

What is your job as a comforter?

_____

_____

Typically, how are the suffering confused about God's comfort?

What is the real reason we suffer?

The removal of personal blame during suffering is a vital step in comforting those who hurt. Why?

When is seeing the end from the beginning possible?

What is the benefit?

Why is it true that we cannot possibly lose?

....

....

....

Summary

Why are some referred to as feeble minded?

....

....

....

13. Support without Strings

Loving Without Expectations

Who are the weak?

_____

_____

_____

What is the difficulty in loving the weak in faith?

_____

_____

_____

How are children often an example of the weak?

_____

_____

_____

When are they capable of returning love?

_____

_____

_____

What implications can be drawn regarding our ministry to the weak in faith?

_____

_____

_____

What is the goal of supporting the weak?

_____

_____

_____

Romans 14

Him that is weak in the faith receive ye, but not to doubtful disputations. For one believeth that he may eat all things: another, who is weak, eateth herbs. Let not him that eateth despise him that eateth not; and let not him which eateth not judge him that eateth: for God hath received him.

Receiving the Weak

The first step in supporting the weak is to receive them without despising them for their weakness. Why is this easier said then done?

_____

_____

_____

What are we to avoid doing?

_____

_____

_____

Describe how Paul dealt with one of these issues.

Describe the above issue.

How do the weak resolve their issues?

Like the other relational skills, supporting the weak starts first inside ourselves. How and Why?

Why is a weak member miserable?

At this point it is critical that we avoid any arguments about the performance issues the weak are depending on for their worth. Why?

....

....

....

....

The question here is not about challenging behavior or setting boundaries, but rather the time and manner in which we go about doing that very thing. How do we do it?

....

....

....

....

Spiritual Enlightenment

How do we see our goal?

....

....

....

The divine intervention needed to change the thinking of those who are weak in the faith is referred to as what?

....

Receiving the weak in the faith is really what?

_____

_____

_____

Supporting the Weak

What does supporting the weak not mean?

_____

_____

_____

What do most of the weak not understand?

_____

_____

_____

What approach does Paul share regarding doubtful issues?

_____

_____

_____

What does anxious preoccupation with their own spiritual condition cause?

_____

_____

_____

What kind of lifestyle does this produce?

....

....

....

Burden Bearing

Supporting the weak may reflect negatively on us. How and Why?

....

....

....

....

What does Paul mean in Galatians 6:2?

....

....

....

What temptation should we avoid when supporting the weak?

....

....

....

Instead what should we encourage them to do?

14. Conclusion

The Role of Faith

When it comes to loving others like Christ our responsibility may be summarized by one word…faith. List the three areas of faith involved.

1.

2.

3.

What is the highest form of worship ?

In contrast to religious rituals what does Paul reveal in Galatians 5:5-6?

In addition to believing, on a daily basis, that we are worthy, what else must we believe?

_____

_____

_____

The Bible is a revelation of who God is and who he has made us to be. What is it not?

_____

_____

Galatians 5:5-6

For we through the Spirit wait for the hope of righteousness by faith. For in Jesus Christ neither circumcision availeth anything, nor uncircumcision, but faith which worketh by love.

How does this answer relate to the question above: In addition to believing, on a daily basis, that we are worthy, what else must we believe?

_____

_____

_____

The Role of Hope

In times of relational strife why is the quality of hope important?

_____

_____

_____

How did Jesus illustrate his unconditional love for his disciples?

Why?

What impact does the love displayed by Jesus have on relational ministry?

About the Author

Jim Groth has been a believer all his life. In his growth as a Christian, God used some difficult life circumstances to help him understand the unique ability of the Gospel to answer many questions about life. Why am I here? What does God want me to do? How can I count on the Grace of God? Who am I, really? How do I relate to God as one who continues to sin? Through a God led sequence of events Jim met John Glenn, the Senior Pastor of Alpha Ministries' "Church in the Woods". Although he was a Christian and understood most of the elements of the Gospel and his faith, Jim found them coalesced to form a better understanding of the whole as he studied "The Alpha Series" presented by John. Finally, his understanding of the Gospel was structured in a way that led to real confidence and meaning.

Subsequently, he joined with John assisting him with publishing The Alpha Series and other publications as well as the Alpha Ministries web site. Jim, a writer himself, has co-authored the Alpha Series Workbook as well as contributed various articles for the *Messenger*, a quarterly magazine published by Alpha Ministries. His passion for the gospel of Jesus Christ has motivated Jim since retiring as a computer programmer and analyst. He lives with his wife, Karen, in Greenville, S. C. where they continue serving the Lord locally.